ANIMALS ON REIKI

Teachings on the Principles of Energy Healing

Books by Nancy Schluntz

Hand in Paw:
A Journey of Trust and Discovery

Animals on Reiki:
Teachings on the Principles of Energy Healing

Also by Nancy Schluntz

"Meeting Sheela Na Gig." In *She Rises*. Vol. 2: How Goddess Feminism, Activism and Spirituality? Edited by Helen Hye-Sook Hwang, Mary Ann Beavis, and Nicole Shaw, pp. 330-334. Mago Books, 2016.

"Big Sister." In *Oh Sister, My Sister: An Anthology of Sisterhood*, edited by Jyoti Wind, pp. 4-5. Starshine Press, 2015.

"Writing, like Breathing." In *The Creative Arc: An Anthology of Writing,* edited by Jyoti Wind, pp. 5-6. Starshine Press, 2012.

"The Drive to Tell the Story." In *Unraveling Mysteries: An Anthology on Women and Aging,* edited by Jyoti Wind, pp. 5-7. Starshine Press, 2011.

ANIMALS ON REIKI

Teachings on the Principles of Energy Healing

Nancy Schluntz

Copyright © 2016 by Nancy Schluntz.

All rights reserved. No part of this book may be reproduced or utilized in any form or by any means, electronic or mechanical, including photocopying, recording, or by any information storage and retrieval system, without permission in writing from the author, except for brief passages in connection with a review.

NOTE: Earlier versions of some of the communications included were published in *Animal Reiki Source* newsletter between August 2013 and March 2015.

Editor: Nancy Carleton, www.NancyCarleton.com

Cover Design: Laura Moyer, www.thebookcovermachine.com

Photographs: All photos licensed from www.istockphoto.com.

Author Photograph: Sean Schluntz, www.wanderingwolfphoto.net

ISBN-13: 978-1537107387; ISBN-10: 1537107380

Library of Congress Control Number: 2016914044

Createspace Independent Publishing Platform, North Charleston, SC.

A portion of the proceeds from sales of this book
will be donated to the
Shelter Animal Reiki Association (SARA),
www.shelteranimalReikiassociation.org.

Important Note

If your companion animal is ill or in pain, please seek veterinary assistance. The services described here are complementary to medical help and are not a substitute for veterinary treatment.

CONTENTS

Foreword xi
Introduction: Curiosity and Exploration 1
Part One, The Precepts: Just for Today 5
   . . . I Will Not Anger 7
      Conversations with Coyote, Skunk,
      Turkey Vulture, and Whale 8
   . . . I Will Not Worry 13
      Conversations with Otter,
      Rabbit, and Boar 14
   . . . I Will Be Humble 19
      Conversations with Bee, Sparrow,
      and Swan 20
   . . . I Will Be Honest in My Work 27
      Conversations with Great Horned Owl,
      Jaguar, and Lynx 27
   . . . I Will Be Compassionate with Myself
and Others 35
      Conversations with Cow and Dolphin 35

Part Two, Another Level 41
   Do Not Bear Anger, For Anger Is Illusion 43
      Conversations with Coyote,
      Dragonfly, and Zebra 43
   Do Not Worry, For Fear is Distraction 51
      Conversations with Great Horned Owl,
      Crane, and Cobra 51
   Be True to Your Way and Your Being 59
      Conversations with Wolf, Tarantula,
      Llama, and Turtle 59

CONTENTS

Show Compassion to Yourself and Others,
for This is the Center of Buddhahood 77
    Conversations with Swan, Penguin,
    and Field Mouse... 77

Conclusion: The Precepts Build
Upon One Another.. 87
    Conversation with Dove 88

Resources 93
Acknowledgments... 95
About the Author 97

FOREWORD

Animals are our teachers and healers. Reiki meditation creates a beautiful healing space where we can more easily awaken to the animal wisdom all around us! For Reiki practitioners, the Reiki precepts are central to our practice of healing and balance.

In this beautiful book, Nancy Schluntz, a dedicated animal advocate and gifted animal communicator and Reiki practitioner/teacher, illuminates the Reiki precepts with teachings from our greatest Reiki teachers, the animals! Large and small, feathered, furry and scaled, animals of all kinds come forward to discuss the Reiki precepts, bringing messages of healing, hope, love and compassion.

This book will change the way you see animals in the world and inspire you to share Reiki with all creatures!

—Kathleen Prasad, Founder,
Animal Reiki Source, and President,
Shelter Animal Reiki Association

INTRODUCTION: CURIOSITY AND EXPLORATION

As an Animal Reiki practitioner, I had often wondered what animals themselves think about the principles that guide Reiki.

Reiki is a Japanese energy healing system originally intended for spiritual development and used today for hands-on or remote rebalancing of energy, which can assist healing. *Rei* means spirit and *Ki* means energy, so the word *Reiki* (pronounced Ray-Kee) translates as "spiritual energy." The nature of Reiki is perfect energetic balance.

Practicing Reiki supports balance and harmony on all levels. It benefits all beings, including animals—domestic and wild, healthy and sick, happy and depressed. All animals—humans and other species—have the ability to bring ourselves back into balance. Reiki energy helps restore that natural balance, from the inside out.

Each being is both teacher and student. The close connection we form with animals while offering Reiki has led me and other practitioners to greater understanding of the Reiki precepts, or codes of practice. Animals have guided practitioners to understand the deeper meanings of freedom from anger and worry; and of humility, honesty, and compassion. You can find many stories of these profound insights in the archives of the *Animal Reiki Source* newsletter and Shelter Animal Reiki Association blogs. Reiki with animals is a two-way process: The animals are recipients of the healing energy, and they're also teachers of the deeper meanings.

In the process of offering Reiki to an animal, many practitioners have discovered that they can feel the animal's feelings, sense the animal's thoughts, and sometimes hear words. The connection woven between animal recipient and human practitioner is one that allows—no, *requires*—the practitioner to set aside preconceptions, assumptions, ego, and all the other quirks that impede our communication with others. Animals help us reach that place of simply *being,* of ego neutrality, which invites the flow of Reiki energy.

The energetic space of ego neutrality is the same in Reiki and in Animal Communication. Years before I began formal training in Animal Communication and Animal Reiki, a turtle and a cat showed me how to step outside of doing and *just be.* The turtle allowed the cat and me to sit by her and witness as she laid her eggs in a burrow she'd dug. In that space of being together, there was awareness of different expressions of life, but no sense of separation.

Curiosity led me to intuitively ask animals to share their perceptions on the first Reiki precept, "Just for today I will not anger." An experiment. I entered into deep meditation with the intention of learning about the Reiki precepts from the animals. The answers that came forth from the animals—each speaking not as an individual but as a representative sharing the wisdom of their species—led me to further sessions and exploration of each of the precepts.

For some of the precepts I had a sense of which animals would be most representative to share wisdom on that topic. Sometimes animals came forward to join the conversation, or were called by other animals. This organic process led to conversations on the first set of Reiki principles, on anger, worry, humility or gratitude, honesty, and compassion. As the conversations and my own practice deepened, I felt the need to have a second set of conversations on the alternate precepts—anger/illusion, worry/distraction, way and being, and a deeper level of compassion. Finally, a summary conversation helped tie it all together.

Reiki energy is universal, and doesn't differentiate according to species. What the animals shared with me will I hope be of service not only to those who offer Reiki to animals but to all who practice Reiki on themselves, on animals, and on other humans. May their wisdom lead you to even greater levels of understanding and practice.

PART ONE

THE PRECEPTS:
JUST FOR TODAY . . .

I will not anger

I will not worry

I will be humble

I will be honest in my work

I will be compassionate with myself and others

. . . I WILL NOT ANGER

"Just for today, I will not anger." The first Reiki precept. When I heard it for the first time, I transmuted the words to ". . . I will not anger others," but then I realized that no one can make anyone else angry. Someone else can be the spark that ignites anger, but the emotion comes from within. This precept is about maintaining the self as a clear conduit for the flow of healing Reiki energy.

Anger has cropped up a lot lately — in news reports, Facebook posts, and other venues. Are people more open now about expressing anger, or is it one of the facets of these times of change?

Do I have anger? I had to think about that. The anger that often calls our attention is the burning, violent kind. The punch-in-the-nose road-rage anger. There are many varieties. Have you ever felt irritated, annoyed, resentful, mistreated, or disrespected, even outraged or filled with righteous indignation? Those are all forms of anger.

In his lecture series *Nonviolent Communication,* Dr. Marshall Rosenberg says that anger is an emotional response triggered by an outside stimulus when a core need isn't being met. Core needs include security, safety, love, nurturance, and yes, respect. When I feel resentment, what need or hurt within me has been disregarded, triggering that feeling?

Conversations with Coyote, Skunk, Turkey Vulture, and Whale

The animals always have responses to such questions. The first to speak was Coyote.

I sensed yellow-gold eyes and tawny fur dancing and feinting around me while Coyote spoke:

Anger is one of my tricks. It distracts your energy and attention. That rush of emotion feels good, feels powerful. When you're caught up in it, you don't recognize that you're being spun away from your purpose, whatever that is. I'm the Trickster. I'm a great teacher, one who teaches you through your mistakes. When you learn to recognize the pull and eddies of my magic and see through them, you can stay on your true path. It's all a game, don't you see? You can follow Coyote and get lost. Or you can say, "Hello, Coyote, I recognize you," and not follow. That strengthens you. When you feel the anger, know that it's my trickster magic at work. Enjoy the thrill of explosion if you wish. Or, this time, ask yourself why you are drawn to my magic. Remember, I teach backward lessons. While you're turned around I'll bite you!

Skunk came next, its parallel white stripes moving in rhythm as Skunk shuffled forward on delicate paws.

My medicine is more about boundaries and respect. Skunk is respected, and respects others. We carry a formidable weapon, but are gentle. We give a warning when we're being encroached upon. We don't release our scent indiscriminately, for then we would be more vulnerable rather than less.

Priorities are important—safety, respect, courage, being gentle. Get your point across without aggression toward self or others. Those we spray recover and learn from the experience to respect us. When you feel anger, learn from us to seek the boundary that's being encroached upon, and address it. Perhaps you won't need to spray at all.

Turkey Vulture flew into our conversation to add its message.

Anger? Rise above it. We soar in the air, the home of spirit and intellect. Rise above the smelly turmoil of emotion. Air helps bring discernment, an ability to sort out cause and effect.

Call on me. I'll help pick away whatever doesn't serve the highest good — whatever doesn't smell right.

Instinctively, I knew that Whale also had a message. Whale said:

Call on me to guide you through the deep waters of emotion. We withstand great pressure in the deep, and rise to the surface to expel old air and breathe in fresh air. Sing our song with us; move with grace and strength. Swim with us, and come up for air.

The animals' messages remind me that the key isn't to deny, bury, or push away anger, but to reach inside myself, locate what has been ignited within, and address that.

These wise teachers offer workable suggestions. Coyote reminds us that when our energy spins off in anger, we diminish our power and lose our focus. Skunk reminds us to respect, be respected, and hold our boundaries. Turkey Vulture reminds us to rise above the smelly stuff and use discernment. Whale reminds us to come up out of the deep emotion and take a breath of fresh air. Thank you, all!

Just for today (just for this hour, just for this moment), I will not anger. I will be a clear vessel for Reiki energy. It takes practice.

...I WILL NOT WORRY

"Just for today, I will not worry." The second Reiki precept. Like the first precept about anger, this one encourages us to be fully present as a clear conduit for the flow of healing Reiki energy.

What is worry but another name for fear? Do we ever worry that things will turn out the way we want them to? No, we just worry that they won't.

We worry when we feel we've lost control, when we fear the unknown, and at times when we face a decision or difficulty and don't know how it's going to turn out. We're anticipating that something unfortunate will happen in the future. Worry creates anxiety, that eating-away-at-your-insides sick feeling.

Paradoxically, when we worry, we're actually pulling energy away from our desired outcome and feeding it toward what we're afraid will happen. Working against ourselves.

The Buddhist proverb on worry is: "If the problem can be solved, why worry? If the problem can't be solved, worrying will do you no good."

It's easy and frustrating to tell ourselves or someone else, "Don't worry." Or in musician Bobby McFerrin's words, "Don't worry, be happy." Yeah, right. Telling ourselves not to worry only adds to the stress of worry—now we're worrying about worrying!

Conversations with
Otter, Rabbit, and Boar

I asked the animals for more specific guidance, and sensed splash, bubbles, sparkles of sunlight through water, movement.

Otter popped up and said, *Why worry? It's all a game. Be flexible. Find joy in each moment, even*

when the unexpected happens. When you worry, you get stiff and solid. That blocks the flow. Worry can make you sick inside, and that's no fun.

Be in gratitude for the abundance that surrounds us. I trust that there will be enough fish for me and my family. If I worry, it drives the fish away and I end up hungry. That's no fun, either. Life is a gift, and everything in it. Just relax and enjoy it.

Have courage, be strong, and set and follow your intentions. Watch as I turn and swim through the water. I waste no energy. When I'm hunting, I'm focused, and I eat. Be sleek like me. Point all your energy in the direction you want to go. It's more fun that way.

Splash! Ripples of water spread out where a moment ago Otter had been.

Next, Rabbit hopped into my meditation:

Ah, fear, Rabbit said. We tremble. We're gentle and we're prey. Our whiskers twitch, sensing, always alert. Walk toward what you fear. Face it. What you fear won't go away. It will linger outside your burrow while you tremble, waiting for you to emerge so it can pounce on you.

Ask yourself, What is it you fear? The great unknowing? It's so human, to want to know everything. You can only prepare as best you can, stay alert and watchful, and be ready to run if you need to—lest you become fear's dinner.

Confronting fear and worry brought Boar to mind.

I heard him snort, *What!*

"Would you share your thoughts about worry with me?"

Worry? Confront it head-on; do your groundwork, focus, and then go forward.

Boar continued: *To worry is to scatter your energy. Prepare, commit, put your head down, and move toward your goal. You can't control what's beyond your reach, but you can prepare for it. Prepare for the unexpected. Focus. Set intention. When you worry, you send mixed signals. You feed energy to what you fear. I didn't get to be this big by scattering my energy all over the field. I know what I want, and I go for it. Sometimes it works, sometimes not. So be it. Snort.* A hoof stomps. Boar's head wags from side to side.

Rabbit, Otter, and Boar give good guidance: Otter reminds us that when we're worrying, it's time to take a break, have some fun, and then focus.

Rabbit reminds us to confront our fear, for it won't go away. Boar reminds us to set our intention and direct all our energy toward it. All say that when we worry, we divert our energy away from our goal and toward what we fear. Worry is a distraction.

We invite worry when our head/mind speaks more strongly than our heart, when we have doubt about the outcome. Prepare as best you can, and then move forward. When we make a mistake, worrying (fretting, stewing) won't fix it. We can only acknowledge and own it, apologize or make amends, and move forward. When worry creeps in anyway, breathe. Let yourself ground deep into the earth. Invite the earth's energy to flow through you with each breath you take, and open your heart. The worry will dissipate. Call on the animals. They're always willing to help.

Just for today, I will not worry.

. . . I WILL BE HUMBLE

"Just for today, I will be humble." The third Reiki precept. Humility is perhaps best defined by what it is not, rather than what it is.

My dictionary defines *humility* as the state or quality of being humble, conscious of our defects or shortcomings; not proud or self-assertive; modest, unpretentious. Humble comes from the Latin *humilis*—low, small, slight, akin to humus, soil, earth. *Humus,* from the Latin for earth, ground, or soil, is the brown or black organic substance resulting from partial decay of plant or animal matter. Humus provides fertilizer for new growth. In my dictionary, *humble* is listed just above *humblebee,* another term for bumblebee. *Humility* comes right above *hummer,* the affectionate term for hummingbirds. It's interesting that the quality of being humble, grounded to the earth, is so closely placed to creatures that fly.

Conversations with Bee, Sparrow, and Swan

I asked to speak with Bee, to gain greater insight into humility. I heard buzzing, and thought to ask if it mattered which kind of bee I spoke with.

The answer came: *No, we're all connected.* Bee continued. *Are we humble? We do our jobs; we move through the world showing how to live cooperatively. We are what we are—no more, no less. Our lives may appear simple to you, yet they are intricate, like our dances. We have disagreements, as do those among your kind. That happens when some lose sight of what's best for the hive. We don't ask for recognition for our work. Nor do we diminish its*

value. Our place in the scheme of things is greater than our size.

Humility is like that. Value the service you do, as part of the greater hive, but don't lose perspective. You have asked me to speak about something that's both very great and very small. Each is an important part of the whole. The whole is diminished when a part is missing, or when a part inflates its own importance. It's delicate—the balance between valuing ourselves and seeking accolades for our growth. When you seek that, it shows that you haven't advanced as far as you think you have. This doesn't apply only to humans, but to all life forms. Balance and being, secure in ourselves. It is enough.

"Thank you, Bee. It's complex, isn't it?"

Bee: *Yes, and no.*

The song of sparrows, who had returned with warmer weather, called my attention outside. Black-crowned and gold-crowned sparrows visit our backyard, with songs that sound lonely and joyous at the same time. I asked to speak with Sparrow.

A soft voice answered, *I am here. It's almost time for nesting. The energies are rising.*

"Thank you for your presence," I said. "Would you share your thoughts about humility?"

Sometimes, Sparrow said, *to be small is to be great, being large and small at the same time. Each being has its place in the scheme of things. Each is important. No more, no less. Some, like the hawks, are larger and have a greater visible impact. Others, like we sparrows, weave the pieces together. Small as we are, we sparrows are an essential part of the web of life. We feed, and we help spread the seeds that bring new life. We're prey and help sustain life for those who are larger. We sing, and our song brings joy.*

Humility is being who you are. Don't measure yourself against others, or make yourself greater or smaller. We don't measure ourselves against the hawks, for theirs is a different journey. Even our flight, undulating up and down, serves to teach that there are higher and lower times. Honor your gifts and use them well. Honor what you receive and be

grateful. Each being has its role. To deny it, or to claim more, damages the whole. We are. That is enough.

Myself, I'm glad to be a sparrow. I love the joy of flight and another season of healthy nesting and the search for food. Think of that joy when you hear our song.

With that, Sparrow flew off to a low branch, and serenaded all who could hear with his beautiful three-note descending call.

Next, I asked to speak with Swan. Swan carries the energy of trust in the future, and an ability to surrender with grace to the will of the universe.

Swan's voice was delicate, gentle, feminine. She said, *Ah, humility. You're familiar with the children's story "The Ugly Duckling"? It's about humility. Even though I could stretch in the pride of my beauty, I swim with my neck bowed for I remember the times of ridicule. The outside appearance, the opinions of others, cannot be a measure of the self. The measure of the self is within. To be humble is to serve, to do our tasks, without undervaluing them or magnifying them.*

I am Swan. Knowing that sometimes I'm awkward and ugly, and sometimes I'm graceful and beautiful, adds to the richness of this life. Humility can be likened to serving the will of the Master to the best of your ability, because the Master asks it of you. Surrender and serve with grace. Honor and responsibility. To serve, when the service is its own reward. When we lose sight of that and claim credit or seek another reward, we diminish the gift of our service. Am I being clear?

You're right in saying that humility is perhaps best defined by what it is not, for being humble is a way of being in the world, free of those aspects of personality that diminish the humility. That sounds complex, but it isn't really. For example, if we claim to be humble, we call attention to it, and therefore we aren't humble, just as when we claim to have reached enlightenment, whatever that is, it only shows that we still have a long way to go to reach that state.

This is an interesting question. It's challenging to place a knowing into the words of language.

I'm grateful to Bee, Sparrow, and Swan, mindful of their gifts. Bees are significant to our health and well-being: Eighty percent of flowering plants rely on bees and other pollinators to reproduce. Sparrow reminds us to see nobility in the most common things, and shows us that through humility we can express unconditional love. Swan reminds us to serve to the best of our ability, without undervaluing or overvaluing our service. All spoke of being great and small at the same time.

Their message of humility in service is guidance for all of us as we grow to trust our inner self, and open to the flow of healing energy that is Reiki. We are in service. That is enough.

Just for today, I will be humble.

... I WILL BE HONEST IN MY WORK

"Just for today, I will be honest in my work." The fourth Reiki precept asks us to be truthfully dedicated to spiritual progress and everything we do. Like the earlier precepts, this one encourages us to be fully present as a clear conduit for the flow of healing Reiki energy.

What exactly does it mean to be fully present?

Conversations with Great Horned Owl, Jaguar, and Lynx

I asked three animals—Great Horned Owl, Lynx, and Jaguar—for their perspectives on the question of honesty in work. Their answers gave me a new perspective on the challenge we humans have with this concept.

With an echo of its call, Great Horned Owl said, *This is a good time, while I'm resting. At night I hunt.*

NANCY SCHLUNTZ

I am the silent hunter. My feathers are silent in flight, so my prey isn't forewarned. The kill is swift. There's no suffering, only an exchange of energies. I take only what I need to survive and to nurture my young. My body, my eyes, my feathers are all in accordance with my role. That is part of the answer to your question.

It's all about focus, and bringing your whole self to your work. Be who and what you are. The sparrows fly an undulating pattern. The vultures soar on thermals and updrafts. Neither attempts to fly as the other. I fly silent and swift among trees, a narrow course full of obstacles, to follow and catch my prey. Vultures can't do this, nor can sparrows. Each has our unique patterns of flight. That's the lesson to apply to your work. Bring your whole self and your unique talents to it, and to the healing and growth that it provides.

Great Horned Owl stretched his wings and talons, and settled on the tree branch before continuing: *A container doesn't hold water if it's full of holes. Showing up is only part of the process. Bringing your full self means being a conduit that's free of leaks. Energy leaks, attention leaks. Any distraction is a leak. As a leak appears, acknowledge it and plug the hole, so to speak. Flying through dense trees requires my full attention. If my attention wanders, I may crash into a branch or miss my prey. It's like that in your work. Focus and be there fully, so that the other may gain the benefit of the healing. That's your concept of honesty in work. Do you understand?*

"I do, Great Horned Owl, and thank you for your wisdom."

Next I asked to speak with Jaguar. A raspy cough announced her arrival. I asked the same questions.

Honesty, Jaguar said, *is being fully yourself in each moment. There's no place for giving only part of yourself. There's no place for "almost" or "not quite." If I didn't bring my full attention, all my senses, my whole body, to my work, I wouldn't eat. I wouldn't survive.*

Some call this concept of honesty in work integrity. The word doesn't matter. The fullness of your attention, your engagement, does matter. With work such as yours, there's the temptation to let the mind wander, to let your focus become blurred. People tell half-truths, shaded truths. We know that humans like to take shortcuts. That isn't honesty. To work with energy as you do and be less than a clear channel isn't honesty.

The efficient use of power is full engagement in the process. Imagine stalking and getting distracted by butterflies! That would mean no meal today. It's not just about the hunt: When I rest, I rest. When I play, I play. When I love, I love. I bring my full self to whatever I'm doing. That's honesty. When I cease to bring my full self to what I do, I will cease to be. That's the rule. Walk in my paws and feel the power of full presence.

Jaguar stretched at the side of the clearing in my meditation, to make room for Lynx.

Lynx emerged from the brush and said, *I've been listening. You're trying to understand honesty from the point of view of the animal kingdom. These are*

artificial concepts to us. We are who and what we are. We bring our full self.

Owl and Jaguar have stated it well. Another word for this quality is commitment. You can sample without commitment. That doesn't lead to healing, *growth, or a full belly. It's an internal standard. Stating the precept, asking the question, showing up, are all good beginnings. It's what happens next that gives it meaning.*

It's humans who need to be reminded of these things. When we hunt, we can't be distracted by thoughts of how hungry we are. It's like that with your work. For people it is not, in most cases, a matter of survival. It's a matter of stretching yourself, of discipline and dedication. Yours is a journey of the mind and what you call spirit. Yet you fill your minds with clutter that is, to us, irrelevant and a distraction. When your mind wanders, your full self is not present. You can ask yourself in each moment, "Am I fully present?" You will know. When you are fully present in any aspect of your life, it will move more smoothly. You learn and grow. If you aren't fully present, you can wander from the path, and even become lost.

For us, there's no halfway. "Almost" would mean death. For people, it's possible to live halfway, not fully present. That's the source of your questions. To live and work fully, dedicated to your pursuits, honestly bringing your full self, is the path to growth. Why would you do otherwise?

I give thanks to Great Horned Owl, Jaguar, and Lynx for sharing their wisdom and perspectives. Great Horned Owl reminds us about focus, and about the reality that each being has unique talents to develop. Jaguar stresses that honesty is bringing your full self to whatever you do. Lynx shares this awareness, and reminds us that we can check in with ourselves at any moment to see if we're fully present, for that's the path to growth.

It's a matter of integrity and commitment—other words for honesty—and of bringing our full self with dedication to this work.

Just for today, I will be honest in my work, and in all my endeavors.

...I WILL BE COMPASSIONATE WITH MYSELF AND OTHERS

"Just for today, I will be compassionate with myself and others." The fifth Reiki precept asks us to "remember the connection among all things within the universe."

Conversations with Cow and Dolphin

A soft, gentle presence and the scent of hay drew close with Cow. I immediately felt comfort in Cow's presence. She said, *I'm familiar with your project. I'm pleased to contribute. It's all for the greater good.*

"Thank you, Cow. Would you share your thoughts on compassion, for self and others?"

Of course. She paused. *You understand that there can't be compassion for others without compassion for self. All are connected. When you offer compassion for others without being compassionate toward yourself, what you offer others is diminished. Each is part of the whole. To value some and not others diminishes the whole.*

"Cow, what is compassion?"

A good question. Kindness, perhaps. Lovingkindness. Respect. You don't need to agree with each part (or person), but refrain from judgment.

Each part of the whole has its role. Some are easier than others, but all have their challenges.

Compassion is also acceptance of our own failings and shortcomings as well as those of others. Hold a standard, yes. Teach and encourage, yes. Love and accept, yes. But don't judge, for we never know the full story of another.

Offering compassion to ourselves is often more challenging than offering it to another, for we may be more critical of ourselves than of others. If all were perfect, there would be no need to live a life. I wouldn't like that, for there would be no grasses to chew, calves to bear, gathering of kindred. Be kind to yourself. Extend to yourself the same kindness — compassion, understanding — that you do to others. The whole will benefit.

"Thank you, Cow. I appreciate your wisdom." Cow breathed her hay-scented breath on me and withdrew.

Then bubbles surrounded me. I heard the clicking of dolphin voices. "Greetings, Dolphin! Welcome to our discussion of compassion."

Dolphin answered: *It's interesting to speak of something that's part of life as we live it — to separate a concept from a way of life. We don't regard what you call compassion as a separate energy. It's part of the flow. For us, the good of the pod is most important. The safety, feeding, and nurturing of the whole. Within the whole are the many parts. Each part has a role. When one of us is ill or damaged, we all swim in support. None can be greater or lesser and maintain the strength and wellness of the pod.*

When you speak of compassion toward self and others, you create a separation between self and others. This works against the well-being of the whole. We know that humans can be very hard on themselves, as if they have forgotten how to play. Some humans give all to others in the name of service, and withhold from self. This would bring weakness to the pod. The pod has health and strength when each member both gives and receives. Each gives in the same measure that each receives. If you don't receive this gift of compassion, then you don't have much to share with others.

The way humans would best benefit from this precept is to remember that the inflow and outflow of these energies must be kept in balance for it to flow fully.

As Dolphin continued, I was aware of the depths of ocean, and sparkling water. *Cow has said that compassion is both loving-kindness and respect. She has put human terms to something greater so that you may understand. What you call compassion is the flow of love, of oneness, that originates with the Source of Life. It's love of the inner being. It's forgiveness and understanding, to use other human terms. To have compassion is to greet each being—including yourself—as a being.*

When you invite this energy to flow through you, it flows best through a clear channel. There's no self and other. There's only the invitation to enter the space of love. You have but a glimpse of the vastness of the resource you call upon. To offer yourself as a portal, a conduit, and feel yourself unworthy, or not to be willing to receive as well, is to diminish what can be shared.

These are concepts that flow together as one wave upon another. To summarize, you need to be willing to give and receive, for then there's balance. To give less, or receive less, diminishes the whole. Is that clear?

I'm thankful to Dolphin and Cow for sharing their thoughts on compassion. Cow reminds us that each is part of the whole of life, all have value, and we never know the full story of another. Dolphin says that to think of ourselves as self and other creates a separation. For there to be balance, we can give to the extent we're willing to receive. Both Dolphin and Cow remind me of the words of Buddhist nun Pema Chodron: "Without loving-kindness for ourselves it is difficult, if not impossible, to genuinely feel it for others."

Just for today, I will be compassionate to all beings—myself and others.

PART TWO

ANOTHER LEVEL

Do not bear anger, for anger is illusion.

Do not worry, for fear is distraction.

Be true to your way and your being.

Show compassion to yourself and others, for this is the center of Buddhahood.

DO NOT BEAR ANGER, FOR ANGER IS ILLUSION

This precept about anger as illusion brings up an internal discussion. More of an argument, really. After studying the first precept, "Just for today I will not anger," I recognized that I do feel anger in some form. Now this precept is telling me that's an illusion? How can that be? The tightening in my body and elevated pulse rate tell me it's real. How can experienced feelings be illusions? Again I turn to the animals for help in understanding.

Conversations with Coyote, Dragonfly, and Zebra

Coyote paused his tap-dance routine on the desert mesa when I connected with him to ask about anger and illusion.

Oh yes, I'm familiar with your project.

"Coyote, are you the right being to ask about this?"

I'm the right being to ask about anything!

I'm the trickster teacher. If I can teach a lesson sideways or backward, that's my way. When you feel anger, ask yourself, why? What is it you expected to happen differently? If there were no expectations, there would be no anger. Expectations are illusion—a mirage of what you want or imagine is real, but it isn't. The anger comes from not being in the moment, from projecting your desires (expectations, illusions) into the future.

"Coyote, I feel like you're leading me in circles."

That's how I teach. What's the fun in following straight lines? Then you expect them to always be straight. See what I mean? When you go in circles or the path is unknown, you can't know where the path will go. When it twists and turns, the stretches of straight path come as a surprise. It's only by following your own internal compass that you can stay on your path.

I'll try every trick I know to confuse you, to divert your focus and energy. When you can recognize my tricks, you're beginning to shift your focus from outside to inside. When I can no longer pull you off center by scattering your energy, confusing and distracting you with illusion, then my teaching will have done its job. That isn't likely to happen, though. Few of you catch on. I have stealth on my side.

"Thank you, Coyote. I appreciate your honesty."

By telling you this I'm not giving away any of my secrets. My tricks are well known. Another level of the game is that people know it's a game but still step backward into playing it. Coyote chuckled. *You know the rules, but you keep playing the game, thinking the outcome will be different. It's only when you stop playing that you will win — you do that by learning the lessons I teach.*

"Thank you, Coyote. You're very wise to the ways of people."

I know. Talk to Dragonfly, too.

Coyote trotted off across the desert sands, searching for the next participant in his game.

A shimmer of insect wings flew into my meditation.

Oh, this is a good story, Dragonfly said. *Illusion is my medicine. I am here, and I am not.* Dragonfly illustrated by flicking in and out of my mind's eye. *My wings are translucent, and also reflect light. My body reflects light. Different wavelengths of light appear as different colors. What color am I? I don't know. I only know that I am.*

From your perspective, I may appear one color or another. I may appear or disappear. It's said we dragonflies can fly between dimensions, but that too is illusion.

When I was a nymph, no world existed above the water's surface. When metamorphosis came, I climbed up the green stalk and in time emerged as a winged creature. What was once the top of my world is now the bottom, for I can linger around water but not go into it. So I'm a creature of both water and air, but not at the same time.

But this lecture on biology doesn't address your question on illusion. Anger is real. It's the result of illusion — something that isn't as it appeared. Or as you wanted it to appear. Illusion is just that. There's no good or bad about illusion. When you expect the illusion to be real, and discover it isn't, or that others hold different illusions about the same thing, then there can be anger. So anger itself is not an illusion, but rather the result of holding an illusion as something fixed or real. Is that clear?

"Yes, Dragonfly. Do you have advice on how we can identify illusion?"

Ah, a good question. Regard all things for and of themselves in each moment. Some things are held by common agreement. Your traffic laws, for example. Your vehicles stop and go according to an agreed-upon set of rules for the greater good. You expect others to abide by those rules. When someone disregards the rules, you sometimes feel anger because the expected behavior wasn't followed.

It's the same with the many small interactions each of you has. Each has a vastly greater set of rules (expectations) that may not have been agreed to by others. Rules that others may not even know you hold. These sets of rules are illusions, yet when they are broken, there can be anger. Disillusionment can be a painful thing.

"Thank you, Dragonfly."

Just remember the teaching—anger is the result of holding an illusion.

With that, Dragonfly shimmered and disappeared.

Then a rustle of tall grass drew my attention as Zebra approached. "Zebra, welcome. Would you like to contribute to this conversation?"

I would. Zebra's voice was low and soft.

Dragonfly spoke of illusion as something which is, and which is not. Coyote likened it to a mirage. I know of this. Our stripes hide us well in the grasses and in the shimmer of summer heat waves. Each Zebra's stripes are unique, yet we appear the same to those who don't know us. It can be hard for a predator to single out one Zebra in the confusion of stripes. You could call us a herd of illusionists. Our appearance distracts and confuses our predators.

What you see isn't always what's there. You don't always see what's there, but often hold illusions about it. When you discover the illusion, you can become angry.

The lioness who hunts us doesn't hold an illusion. She knows that within the herd of stripes there's a weaker or slower one, and that one becomes her target. She doesn't expect her prey to stand still and wait for her claws; she only knows that she has a better chance of bringing down the weak one. Her focus is on her mission of securing food.

When your focus is steady on your purpose, the illusions won't so easily distract you. Anger is disillusion turned inward. When you bear anger toward another, it's because the other didn't comply with your illusion. You might bear anger toward yourself for holding the illusion. Either way, you suffer.

To bear anger also implies carrying weight. If I were weighted down, I couldn't run as fast to escape my predators.

The amount of anger you carry is proportional to the amount of illusion you hold. How great is the burden you carry? To set that weight down, to release it, lightens your step, your energy, your being. It's a lot healthier!

Remember, not everything is black-and-white. Sometimes it only appears so. That's illusion.

"Thank you, Zebra!"

Zebra withdrew into the grasses of the savannah, her stripes blending with those of her herd and the shimmer of summer heat.

Coyote, Dragonfly, and Zebra share great wisdom on different aspects of this precept. Coyote teaches that the only way to win the game of misdirection that results in anger is not to play the game. Dragonfly explains how we hold many illusions, often without knowing it, and experience anger when the illusions are found to be just that—illusions. Zebra shares that focus dispels illusion, and that bearing anger makes us vulnerable.

Anger can also grow out of a sense of helplessness. When the spark of anger flashes, or its coals smolder, the key is to look within to find what ignited it. What fuel burns within?

Do not bear anger, for anger is illusion.

DO NOT WORRY, FOR FEAR IS DISTRACTION

In the first set of precepts, the animals teach that worry gives energy to what is feared. They encourage us to *focus*. Now we turn to "Do not worry, for fear is distraction." This precept reminds me how often my attention follows random thoughts that float through my mind in meditation. Distractions shift focus. There will always be distractions, fears, worries, to-do lists, and myriad other calls on my attention. It takes practice to set intention, to bring my full self to the present moment, to focus, and to hold it there. With practice, though, we can find that inner stillness that doesn't sway with wind and current, and we can hold it for longer periods. The animals show us how.

Conversations with Great Horned Owl, Crane, and Cobra

Great Horned Owl blinked his great golden eyes and ruffled his fathers.

"Owl, would you share your thoughts about the precept 'Do not worry, for fear is distraction'?"

What you speak of is focus. Focus on your goal. When I spot prey, I focus on it and fly for it. Even when it's in the grip of my talons, I don't lose my focus, for the hunt isn't complete until the food is consumed.

If I were to worry about which way to approach, or whether the prey would escape, my focus would be diminished, and with it my skill as a hunter.

Energy follows thought. When you worry, you're really in fear that what you seek won't be attained—and by allowing that, you diminish your chances of success. You've given energy to the outcome you fear.

Thus yes, fear is a distraction. It takes focus away from your goal. And worry is another name for fear.

Just follow my example. Set your focus, have confidence in your skills, and don't be distracted by other possible outcomes. Sometimes I'm not successful, but that's because in the dance of hunter and hunted sometimes the hunted wins. It's all about balance.

To learn more about balance, talk to Crane.

""Thank you, Owl. I appreciate your wisdom."

Any time, Great Horned Owl said, and settled back onto his tree branch.

A stillness came over my meditation. A great white crane stood motionless, balanced on one slender leg. When I connected with Crane, she stretched the black leg that had been folded under her body, and took a step in the shallow water.

"Crane, Great Horned Owl and I were talking about how worry is fear and a distraction. He suggested I talk with you about balance."

Yes, I know. When will you learn that your thoughts precede you? I knew you would call on me and have been listening.

"Thank you, Crane. It's a lesson I keep learning over and over."

Crane felt no need to acknowledge what was obvious. She continued: *Balance is achieved when you are centered within, neither pulled to front or back, right or left. That's another way to look at focus. When your focus is within, in your center, you can stand as I do, in perfect balance. The breeze can ruffle my feathers, the current can tug at my leg, but I*

don't let it pull me off center. If I were to worry about falling, my focus would be dispersed and I would have difficulty standing as I do.

When I move, I walk with steady grace. The fish don't sense danger, for my legs are much like the sea grass. My spearing movement is quick. When I fly, there's efficiency of movement. No energy is wasted splashing or flapping about. I teach balance through the way I move. You would do well to study my movements.

"Thank you, Crane. So you say that to keep balance, we need to keep focus within our center and not be pulled off center by winds and currents—or by worries and distractions."

Correct.

Crane returned to her one-legged stance in the inlet, her body turned to face into the breeze.

I pondered Crane's lesson about balance, and Great Horned Owl's lesson about focus. Discernment came to mind. Was discernment a key to both?

The image of Cobra came to me — coiled, with regal head raised.

Yesssss?

"Cobra, we have been discussing worry, fear and distraction. It seems to me that discernment is an element in that concept."

True. We snakes have to discern when to advance and when to withdraw, when to strike and when to be still, which prey are ready to offer themselves and which are not. No wasted energy.

To answer your question: Your intent must be clear. In order to focus, you must know where to place that focus. Discernment is necessary, for there are many alternative paths. One will take you where you want to travel; other paths won't.

Discernment aids in keeping focus, as well. Just as balance requires many minute, almost imperceptible corrections—similar to how Crane's winds and tides push and pull her—discernment helps sort new information. Owl, for example, spoke of focusing on his prey. If he focused only on that prey's location, grasp of his talons would be futile if the prey moved moments before the strike. Discernment allows for the consideration of changing information.

This isn't the same as being distracted by an alternate goal or feared outcome. That kind of distraction—worry born of fear—pulls energy away and upsets focus and balance. Worry adds strength to that which you fear.

If, for example, you were to begin to fear that I would strike you, delivering my deadly poison into your arm, that's the picture I would see. It would be like an invitation: "Here, strike at my arm!"

I don't think that's what you want. It is, however, a good example of how worry distracts from the focus of intention.

"Thank you, Cobra. I hear your lesson and respect your wisdom."

Cobra nodded, and withdrew, barely moving the tall grasses.

I'm grateful to Great Horned Owl, Crane, and Cobra for sharing their wisdom and perspectives. Just as this precept expands upon the earlier version of "Just for today, do not worry," Great Horned Owl's instruction about focus, Crane's advice on maintaining balance, and Cobra's wisdom on discernment add great clarity.

Do not worry, for fear is distraction. Set your intention, stay focused, and use discernment to adjust your path and balance; don't be distracted or send energy to that which you fear.

Solid advice for us all!

BE TRUE TO YOUR WAY AND YOUR BEING

So many questions. What do *way* and *being* mean? When pondering a question or concept, I've learned to refer back to an earlier concept. A clue is that there are five precepts in the first set, and four in the second set. This precept brings together the teachings about being humble and being honest in your work, and takes those teachings to a new level. The animals come forth to explain.

Conversations with Wolf, Tarantula, Llama, and Turtle

The voice said: *Be true and follow your inner compass. Don't be blown off track by the opinions and demands of others.*

The Way in Buddhism is the Dharma, the teachings. The Way in Christianity is how Jesus taught.

The Way for each person is where your compass feels strong and well calibrated, with body, mind, and soul in alignment.

I asked, "Who are you? Can you help me understand?"

Wolf replied: *Who are you? You are many things —the sum of all you have learned and experienced.*

Do you know that I am with you all the time?

"No."

Don't be so timid. That invites others to see you are prey. You're a more advanced student than you realize! I have therefore dispensed with the introductory formalities.

The power of Wolf's presence felt bristly, like guard hairs standing on end.

I have much more to teach you, but for now I'll limit my instruction to your topic: Be true to your way and your being.

This seems like a simple thing, but it's fraught with distractions. Primary among them is not having a clear vision of your way or your being. It's hard to be true to something when you don't see clearly what it is.

The first step is to align in your center. That is, your own center — not one of another's choosing, nor what you "ought" to think or feel, but rather what comes from the core of your self. To illustrate, when we hunt, there are many scents — some quite delectable — that entice us away from the track of our quarry. But if we want to eat, we must focus on the primary goal. We become one with the hunt.

The equivalent for you in this context is to "Be Reiki," to be aligned with the precepts and in a place of neutrality from which you do not anger, or worry, or judge. There's great joy in moving smoothly in the oneness.

Your being is the true core of your self — the sum total of all you have learned and experienced, all you have suffered and forgiven. It's that place of humility and gratitude, where love is pure and asks nothing, yet is open to receive.

I thought then of J. Allen Boone's book *Kinship With All Life,* and the slowly learned lessons within it.

Wolf continued: *Yes,* kinship *is a good term for it. When you're true to your own being, you're in kinship with all life. There's no hierarchy, only different paths. To be true to your way is to honor and follow the path you have chosen, or that has chosen you. The manner of choosing isn't important, so long as there's resonance. Don't waste time and energy choosing a path that isn't right for you.*

You think of the term lone wolf *as a loner, isolated, but what this means to us is for each to be in alignment with his or her true nature. Yet we live in community and are family oriented within a community that comes together by choice for our mutual good.*

There I think you have the core of it. There's much more — many perspectives. Remember that with true strength comes gentleness. This isn't a cloak that you put on and take off, but a way of walking through the world, one paw print, one hunt at a time. Being true to yourself can be hard at first, as you learn who that self is and the false selves fall away. Then it becomes smoother, like running when you have found your rhythm.

They go together — learning your way and your being. They help each other. Tarantula can tell you more about that.

"Thank you, Wolf! I'm grateful."

Yes. Wolf had finished his lesson, his teaching for this encounter, and withdrew.

Movement caught my attention. I watched in awe as the large, hairy Tarantula made her way forward.

Tarantula's voice sounded young and old, near and far away, almost with an echo. She chuckled.

That's because I am such an ancient creature, the star of many legends. I'll consolidate my energy for you.

"Thank you."

Tarantula continued: *Wolf called me to help answer an aspect of your question.*

I thanked Tarantula. She stood before me in my meditation clearing. I'm not afraid of spiders, and regard them with great respect. This one, though, was in my mind's eye the largest I'd ever imagined, standing as tall as I was as I sat cross-legged on the sand.

Tarantula, hearing my thoughts, chuckled again, then continued:

Part of this being true to your way and your being is about trust. Trust in your own intuitive sense of what that is. Trust in your teachers and your own discernment process. If something doesn't feel quite right, examine it. Why doesn't feel right? Is it counter to an earlier lesson? Then evaluate both in the light of truth. Sometimes we have lessons that guide us for a period, but we outgrow them. For example, so many humans carry the teaching "I'm not worthy." Then, when you experience true and pure love, you may have a tendency to deflect or deny that love because you don't feel worthy. Perhaps it's time to discard the too-tight skin of "not worthy" and let yourself be loved. But I'm not here to discuss esoteric faith and belief systems, even though your question lends itself to that.

The basic question is to review each and every belief, and even each teaching that you hold. Look at it in the light, and discern if this belief or teaching is in alignment with the internal compass of which Wolf spoke earlier.

Your true being is to be in alignment with that compass. Your way is to move through the world while staying in alignment with that way of being.

That sounds convoluted, but it isn't. Picture an orb spider spinning its web, focused, knowing the pattern beforehand, stepping lightly across the web as it grows. The spider is the web; the web making is the spider.

For me, as a tarantula, I also bring the lesson of releasing what no longer fits. When your beliefs and actions — the things you have learned — constrain your movement and growth, it's time to break free. Release yourself from them. If you insist on believing you're not worthy, or not good enough, how can you grow into your full potential?

We tarantulas grow, and when our casing becomes too tight, it cracks. We shed. Stepping out of the old casing is liberating, and at the same time frightening. To breathe deeply, and know for a time you're vulnerable. It's like when you spoke with Snake in an earlier conversation. A casing serves to support and protect, but to grow means releasing that casing and growing a larger one. This is all part of growth and transition.

It comes back to trust. Trust in your instincts, your growth, your discernment about what serves your growth and what's no longer a good fit. This applies to shell casings as well as thoughts, beliefs, and actions. The patterns of your life. When something no longer fits, have the courage to break free from it, for the sake of your own growth, for your own growth is part of your being and your way.

Note that as a tarantula I'm a spider, yet I live in a burrow. Other kinds of spiders weave webs. Each weaves its own distinct kind. We are each true to our own nature, and our own way. It all comes back to a rather neat circle, doesn't it?

"Yes, it does, Tarantula. You've made it very clear. Thank you for sharing your wisdom."

I sensed another animal being waiting to add to the conversation—Llama.

The brown-and-white spotted llama began: *Yes, it is I who was with my cria at Machu Picchu.*[1] *Thank you for your courtesy that day.*

"I'm sorry I wasn't more effective in influencing the other people to be more considerate of you."

You were effective. You helped and supported me. I give you now to our Speaker, the one who speaks for us.

I saw a black llama with tassels of colorful Andean yarn strung from his ears.

Llama: *Your question?*

"I'm inquiring about the precept 'Be true to your way and your being.'"

Llama: *Ah yes. That one. Think of yourself as one of us, making your way along a narrow path or ledge, or along a trail with slippery rocks. Place your feet well. Know where they are. Don't carry too*

---

[1] The exchange Llama references here is described in my book *Hand in Paw: A Journey of Trust and Discovery*. Chapter "Return to Peru," print edition, p. 351, 2014.

heavy a load. Others will try to overload you if they can, but don't allow it! It is enough to carry your own load. Don't carry the burdens of others. Those burdens will pull you off track.

Be true to your own way! [Llama made a point of emphasizing your *own* way.]

Not the way dictated to you or imposed upon you by others. Your chosen way. That isn't to say that your way won't change as you learn more and come to branches in the path. Discernment is necessary. The key is to be true to your own way, not that of others. Be true to the path you have chosen. In the context of the practice associated with this teaching [Reiki], this means to be true to the teachings, not to diverge, not to become distracted and wander from the path, for that's how you get lost. Keep coming back to the center.

This leads to being true to your being. Know who you are, in the very center of your being. This sets your internal compass. We stand tall and serve, but we don't let anyone overload or abuse us. When you know who you are, and your internal compass is set, you can stay on your path. In the same manner, staying on your path, your way, helps strengthen your being. This sounds like a circle, and it is. As you grow and learn and practice, your sense of being will also grow. It's like the cycle of being shorn—the sense of lightness that follows shearing, followed by a new cycle of growth. I don't mind giving my growth to people, for it benefits them, keeps them warm, and promotes creativity.

As you grow, you may discern that some of the teachings you have followed no longer serve you. You've grown beyond them. We grow in stages and cycles for a reason.

When it's time to release a way that no longer serves your growth, release it. We llamas do that by allowing ourselves to be shorn. Tarantula referred to it as stepping out of a too-tight casing. You may find that your path needs some adjustments. Discern within if a change is in alignment with your internal compass, or if it's a distraction. Keep coming back to your center.

Think of us llamas as we step lightly and surely on the trails, loads balanced, heads held high. We're all here to grow and to serve. How that growth and service takes place is your individual path. Stand in your center, discern your path, and place your feet firmly upon it.

Winds will blow, shortcuts will beckon, and sometimes others will try to get you to carry their load. Remember to be true to your own way, your own path. It gets easier with practice.

"Llama, I feel this wisdom goes beyond an explanation of a precept. It's more of a lesson in living."

Llama: *See, you're learning already! Take what I've said, consider it, hold it up to your internal compass, and discern the deeper meanings.*

I'll let you sit with that for a while before we move on to other topics another time.

"Thank you, Llama."

With a click of hooves on rock, Llama was gone.

Then I heard the slight scrape of Turtle's claws as she made her way across the dirt path, pausing to nibble at a green sprout.

She asked, *Don't you know I'm always with you?*

"Yes, Turtle, though sometimes not front and center."

That's the way of it.

"Turtle, would you please share your thoughts about 'Be true to your way and your being'?"

Turtle chomped on a blade of grass and thought for a moment. *Some are faster than I, and some are slower. I move at my own pace. I don't try to keep up with others, although I can move surprisingly fast when I need to!*

This precept teaches you to honor your full self —to bring your inner self out into the world in whatever you do. Others may call it walking your talk.

I don't need a lot. Food and water, shade and sun. I retreat into my shell to protect myself and to conserve energy. I emerge to seek nourishment and companionship. I speak now as a being who lives on both land and water. Others of my kind live only in water or on land. Yet we have the same expression of turtleness.

"What is the way of Turtle?"

We are steadfast; we move toward our objective at our own steady pace. We protect ourselves, and pause to nourish ourselves when needed.

Many of your legends speak of us as the center of grounding. One foot at a time, close to the earth, neck extended, we move forward. We help one another. When one of us is stuck, another will help right us.

You want to ask about the being of Turtle. They are the same. The way is being; being is the way.

"Is this the same as honoring your true self?"

When your thoughts and actions, your energies, are expressions of your inner self, your way and being are the same. I don't put on and take off my shell — the outer part of me — whenever I feel like it. Inner and outer are one and the same. Humans often change their behavior depending on whom they are with or where they are. Why is that? What is the real you?

This precept helps you to be a constant, steady expression of who you are — the being within. For humans, coming to this place is a life journey. It might help you to remember what I teach as you study this precept: Move at your own pace, honor your own cycles, be an outward expression of your interior self, and nurture and protect yourself as circumstances require.

With that, Turtle turned and made her way back up the path, her clawed feet scraping the dirt with each step. Her domed shell blended with rocks on the path until she appeared as one of them, reminding me of how ancient Turtle is.

While transcribing these conversations, I began to feel that this precept was related to intention, and asked to speak again with Wolf.

Wolf approached—tall, long legs, palpable presence.

"Wolf, may I ask you more?"

Of course.

"I have more questions about this precept of way and being. Is it related to intention?"

Yes. You're learning! To set intention is to set your path, and to bring your energies into focus on that path. In the context of the work—the energy work of Reiki—it's to focus all of your being on that intention. *The clearer the intention, the more effective the process.*

When you say "Be Reiki," you've created the intention to follow that path and adhere to it in all your activities. This can be for the duration of a session or a lifetime. With practice you can deepen so that your core is aligned.

When we speak of a way, it can be a path of travel, growth, or a way of being. So the alignment is both the way and the being.

We spoke earlier of the compass. When the alignment is true, it can be felt throughout the whole being. The precept doesn't say way or being, but way *and* being. *They are one and the same.*

So, yes, when you set your intention for each process, for each day, your way and your being are aligned. *If you allow slippage around the edges, you become out of alignment.*

"How can I be sure I'm being true to my way and my being?"

You'll feel it. Set your intention. Focus. You'll feel whether or not the alignment is true. It takes practice. Our cubs aren't born knowing how to track and hunt. They begin learning through play and by watching their teachers. We demonstrate for them and they learn that way.

Choose your teachers well. Sometimes it's necessary to work with a teacher who isn't aligned, so you'll learn to feel the difference when you move on to one who's well aligned. It's all in the growth and learning.

I remembered the animals telling me that all beings are on a path of growth—including our teachers!

Wolf: *So keep practicing, set clear intentions, and be true to your way and your being—even as that way develops and your being grows and stretches. It's all part of the flow.*

"Thank you, Wolf. I appreciate your wisdom."

Wolf: *You may call on me again.*

Wolf left me to continue my meditation.

Wolf teaches that our way and being are the way we move through the world, and to be true to our chosen path, and do it with intention. Tarantula speaks of trust, and the need to review and evaluate every belief and teaching, measuring them against the internal compass that she and Wolf describe. Llama reminds us to stay in our center, discern our path, and place our feet firmly upon it. Llama also reminds us about holding good boundaries. Turtle teaches us to move at our own pace, honor our own cycles, be an outward expression of our interior self, and nurture and protect ourselves.

These animals' wisdom stresses that being true to our way and our being is coming to the center of ourselves and expressing that in all behaviors. It's not something we put on and take off.

I'm grateful for these teachings as I continue to absorb the information long after the teacher animals withdraw.

SHOW COMPASSION TO YOURSELF AND OTHERS, FOR THIS IS THE CENTER OF BUDDHAHOOD

This precept has also been translated as "Show compassion to yourself and others because this is the center of the universe." The use of *Buddhahood* here refers to a state of enlightenment rather than a spiritual or religious tradition. In the previous precept about compassion, we are reminded that in order to be compassionate with others, we must also have compassion for ourselves. Now, the animals show us how to go deeper.

Conversations with Swan, Penguin, and Field Mouse

Ripples on the water's surface broke sunlight into a scattering of golden reflections.

Swan began: *So much of compassion is about not judging. Being who you are, learning the lessons of life, understanding. You're familiar with the story of the Ugly Duckling. We've talked of it before. Now people call me beautiful, which carries its own expectations. If I were to appear less than graceful, I'd be judged for not meeting the viewer's expectations. This is harmful to both me and the viewer.*

Compassion is to understand that each being is on its own path of growth. One being's path cannot be compared to another's. Each soul's journey unfolds in its own way and time. Don't measure another's journey by your own, or your own by another's.

Compassion is like the smooth surface of the lake upon which I glide.

Talk to Penguin, and then come back to me.

"Thank you, Swan."

Penguin was waiting. *Compassion is recognizing that each being has a role. Some roles are to help other beings learn their life lessons. The base of the totality of existence is love. Each has a role in the great fabric of life.*

Swan said that compassion is to refrain from judging and comparing. Those are such human traits.

Compassion is a way of being. It's unencumbered by anger, fear, or jealousy—all of those emotions that distract from the essence. In fact, if you carry any of those emotions, your ability to feel compassion is limited.

The other part is compassion toward self. If you don't have compassion for self—true love for self—your ability to hold it for others is limited.

The term Buddhahood *comes from the same source as these precepts. Similar teachings emerge from other traditions, such as "Love one another as I have loved you." It's an expression of recognition of the oneness of All That Is. This is going more into the philosophy of faith traditions, but you understand what I mean. All life is connected. To judge or disparage a part of the web of life weakens the web upon which all stand.*

Part of the teaching is to be at peace, with yourself mostly. If you equate compassion with love, it follows that you can't fully love another unless you love yourself. There's a give-and-take, an ebb and flow to being, like breathing. We slip through the water because we don't resist it. We are at one with the water. When you're at one with another—with

their essence, not just their outward presentation—there's that same flow.

When we walk on land, our waddle is often regarded by humans as clownish. We don't take this in, for we know that this is but one aspect of our being. Yet those who think us clownish on land also witness the grace and ease with which we move through water. Both aspects are part of who we are, and we hold that knowing. If we allowed the opinions of others to guide our behavior, we would spend all of the time being graceful in water. Then we could never reproduce. The key is to look within yourself and others, and honor that essential being, not just judge and form expectations based on one of the aspects. All are necessary parts of the whole, and each being is on its own journey. So don't be so hard on yourself. And have some fun!

With that, Penguin launched himself down an ice sheet, tobogganing his way to the ocean.

I called after him, "Thank you, Penguin!"

I was still smiling as I returned to Swan.

Swan showed me a picture of herself flying, neck and wings outstretched, at ease in air as Penguin is in water.

Do you see? she asked. *People are most familiar with my image on water, yet I'm am a being of air and of land. Three realms call forth three different aspects of me. Yet all are one. I am what I am, yet I appear different in different circumstances. Don't allow your perceptions—of yourself or others—to cloud your understanding of the essential self of each being.*

Each being is on a journey of growth. Some are aware of it, some aren't. You can find some expressions of that growth uncomfortable or distasteful, and still have compassion for the being within. The same is true for yourself. You humans are so hard on yourselves! Always judging, measuring, and falling short. It may help to remember that a bird such as I has many feathers. Each feather serves a purpose. The totality of feathers also serves a purpose.

That's getting a bit far afield. Just remember that the being within you and the beingness within others are all bright sparks of the great web of life, the All That Is. be kind to yourself and others. Love really is *all there is.*

With that, Swan fell silent, giving me time to absorb and record her words.

I felt a deepening of my own humility and a warmth that expanded outward from my heart. "Thank you, Swan."

She nodded, and said: *There's one other to speak with.*

A rustle in the grass attracted my attention. A soft brown head with round ears appeared, and small dark eyes blinked at me. The field mouse sat up on his hind legs and regarded me, whiskers twitching.

Compassion, is it? said Mouse. *For self and others? Buddhahood? All names for being a willing part of the oneness. So many regard us as pests and seek to destroy us, but others value us. Yes, we eat crops and grain. We also burrow and help the earth to breathe. We're small, yet we can overcome much greater challengers. We're teachers—how many stories have been written about us? We're an essential part of the chain of life.*

We're both honored and reviled. Yet we go about our work, holding these in balance. We rodents, and our colleagues the insects, come in many forms, each with a purpose—like Swan's feathers. None is greater or less than another. When you lack compassion for yourself or another, it diminishes the whole. To have compassion—true compassion—for any being strengthens the whole.

The web of life is so much greater than any can imagine, and all parts of it are connected. It matters not how.

Each is a valued and essential part of the whole. Each has a purpose. No one knows the extent of another's journey. The journeys can be vastly different, but within each is a being. Recognize that being, including the one within yourself.

I found myself marveling at the great wisdom coming from this small mouse.

Ah, he retorted, *see what I mean? You just held an expectation of my wisdom and capability based on my physical size.*

"Yes," I said, and found my focus shifting. The bright being within Mouse and the one within me connected, one being to another.

It was good.

Penguin yelled *Wahoo!* and dove into the water. Swan stretched and flapped her wings, then tucked them at her sides, each feather in its place.

I felt something shift within me, and gave thanks to each for sharing their wisdom and perspectives with me.

Swan reminds us to not measure our being's journey by another's, and not to allow our perceptions to cloud our understanding of the essential self of each being. Penguin tells us that compassion is a way of being unencumbered by anger, fear, or jealousy. *In fact,* he adds, *if you carry any of those emotions your ability to feel compassion is limited.* Field Mouse points out that his kind is both honored and reviled, yet they go about their work holding those perceptions in balance. Each has a purpose, and no being is greater or less than another: *The web of life is so much greater than any can imagine, and all parts of it are connected. It matters not how.*

Show compassion for yourself and others, for this is the center of Buddhahood.

CONCLUSION: THE PRECEPTS BUILD UPON ONE ANOTHER

The Reiki precepts are listed in a specific order:

> For today only . . .
>
> I will not anger
>
> I will not worry
>
> I will be humble
>
> I will be honest in my work
>
> I will be compassionate with myself and others

Or, stated another way:

> Do not bear anger, for anger is illusion.
>
> Do not worry, for fear is distraction.
>
> Be true to your way and your being.
>
> Show compassion to yourself and others, because this is the center of Buddhahood

As I've studied the precepts and listened to what the animals had to say about each of them, I've come to better understand their depth and how they work together. They build one upon another.

Conversation with Dove

I asked Dove for further clarity. A flutter of wings, a calm presence, and Dove said, *I am here.*

"Dove, would you share your thoughts on the cumulative nature of the Reiki precepts?"

Oh yes, Dove said. *It's often not until you begin to practice compassion that you understand it's only possible after working with the preceding precepts.*

Anger doesn't allow compassion, for self or others.

Worry shows a lack of faith or trust in the flow of all things. To trust releases your need to control and allows acceptance of what is.

These first two are the foundation upon which the others can be built. The structure of the nest, so to speak.

Humility—true humility—is the beginning of growth. Humility is like the soft down that lines and insulates a nest. It's the place where the heart rests.

Honesty is like the eggs I lay in my nest. To be honest is to bring your full self, to accept responsibility. To thrive, the eggs must be kept warm, turned, and protected. To see them to hatching requires attentive nurturance.

After hatching, the chicks need to be protected and nurtured. The parents need to feed themselves first in order to be able to feed the hatchlings. We nurture them as they fledge and, in their time, take flight. This is how compassion flows. It begins with the self and then extends outward. Feed yourself, nurture your offspring, and encourage them to fly so their cycles may continue. Thus compassion spreads through the world.

Then rest. Another cycle begins. All is flow, and in time the nest must be repaired or a new one built. Outside forces, or distractions, such as weather and predators, keep us constantly alert. There's no completing a cycle and then stopping, for everything is in constant motion. So be alert and attentive! Circumstances may arise that cause you to feel anger, or to worry. That weakens the structure of your nest.

Compassion is active, not passive. It may feel gentle, like the softness of a down feather, but that's because discordant anger and worry are absent. Humility is the key, the place of the heart. From there honesty and compassion can grow. To live by these precepts, you need to continually inspect the strength of your nest, the softness of the down insulation, your attention and focus, and nurture yourself as well as others.

Pay attention to the cycles within yourself, and to the cycles of nature. Within is the continuous cycle of nest building, egg laying, hatching, and free flight. Each depends on the phase before. So it is with your Reiki precepts. They are a living cycle within you. You cannot be in alignment with the precept of compassion without being in alignment with the precepts that come before it. You cannot be in compassion until you have released anger, and fear or worry. When you have learned humility, and honesty, then you can be in compassion, for you have gained understanding of the path of living. Living isn't easy, but it can bring great joy.

"Thank you, Dove. I appreciate how clear you've made the relationship among the precepts, and your understanding and insights."

I'm left to think about the wisdom of the animals, and how we learn from them by watching their interactions and the cycles of nature. A tree is a good example of these precepts in motion. A tree grows from a seed to a sapling to a mature tree within the cycles of nature. A tree isn't composed of roots, trunk, and branches like blocks stacked one on top of another, just as the Reiki precepts don't function as stacked blocks. The flow of growth is cyclical and continuous. Just as Dove describes the cycle of a nest, and just as a tree illustrates the cycles of growth, we deepen in our understanding of the Reiki precepts as we practice them. It's a continuous process of learning, deepening, and growth.

Great teachers surround us.

We just need to pay attention.

RESOURCES

Boone, J. Allen. *Kinship with All Life.* HarperOne, 1976.

Prasad, Kathleen. *Shoden and Animal Reiki Training: The Basics*, manual. Animal Reiki Source, 2015.

Prasad, Kathleen. *Okuden and Animal Reiki Training: Advanced Techniques*, manual. Animal Reiki Source, 2015.

Prasad, Kathleen. *Shinpiden and Animal Reiki Teacher Training*, manual. Animal Reiki Source, 2015.

Rosenberg, Marshall. *Nonviolent Communication: A Language of Life.* PuddleDancer Press, 2003. Recording available from www.Soundstrue.com.

Schluntz, Nancy. *Hand in Paw: A Journey of Trust and Discovery,* Createspace, 2014.

Santideva, Acarya (attributed), Buddhist proverb. In Vesna A. Wallace and B. Allan Wallace, Translators, *A Guide to the Bodhisattva's Way of Life.* Snow Lion, 1997.

Steinberg, Eden, editor, *The Pocket Pema Chodron.* Shambala Pocket Classics, 2008, p. 41.

Stiene, Frans and Bronwen. *Shinpiden Level III: Mystery Teachings*, manual. International House of Reiki, 2010.

The following resources helped provide guidance on which animals to call upon for interviews:

Andrews, Ted. *Animal Speak: The Spiritual and Magical Powers of Creatures Great and Small.* Llewellyn Publications, 1993.

Farmer, Steven D. *Animal Spirit Guides.* Hay House, 2006.

Sams, Jamie, and David Carson. *Medicine Cards* book. St. Martin's Press, 1988–1989.

ACKNOWLEDGMENTS

I'm grateful to Leah D'Ambrosio of SARA, the Shelter Animal Reiki Association, for her encouragement to write the first set of animal communication interviews about the Reiki precepts, and to Kathleen Prasad for her dedication to teaching Animal Reiki (www.animalReikisource.com). Thanks also to Frans Stiene, Reiki Master/Teacher and cofounder of the International House of Reiki (www.ihReiki.com).

My appreciation to Cindy Comer and her dogs, Blue and Rusty; and to Thena MacArthur and her cat in spirit, Mac, for their willingness to be interviewed for this book. Unfortunately, that section was removed as I tightened the book to focus on its core message about the Reiki precepts. Their comments will be included in another work.

Thanks to my editor, Nancy Carleton, for bringing consistency to this writing, and for catching my tendency to capitalize Important Words.

Thanks also to Genie Lester and the Wednesday Writers, who listened to and offered helpful suggestions on sections of this work.

Heartfelt thanks and blessings to the animals who came forth to share the wisdom of their species with all of us. The animals are great teachers; we only need ask, and listen. And to the people who participate in this work, blessings on your way.

ABOUT THE AUTHOR

Rev. Nancy Schluntz is a Reiki III (practitioner/teacher) SARA member and Animal Communicator. As an Animal Chaplain, she offers pet-loss bereavement counseling and facilitates a pet-loss support group. She specializes in helping animals and their people through times of transition, such as adoption, rehoming, relocating, death, and changes in family configuration. Nancy also offers Reiki to animals at the wildlife rehabilitation center where she volunteers. She has written an inspirational memoir, *Hand in Paw: A Journey of Trust and Discovery* (available on Amazon). Her blog, with messages from animals, nature, life's journey, and world religions, can be found at:

www.NancySchluntz.com.

Nancy follows the Animal Reiki Practitioner Code of Ethics as developed by Kathleen Prasad, Founder of the Shelter Animal Reiki Association (SARA) and Animal Reiki Source.

Made in the USA
San Bernardino, CA
11 April 2017